Cambodian Girls

Hot Sexy Cambodian Lingerie Girls Models Pictures

By **PHOTO ART LOVER**

Copyright © Cambodian Girls

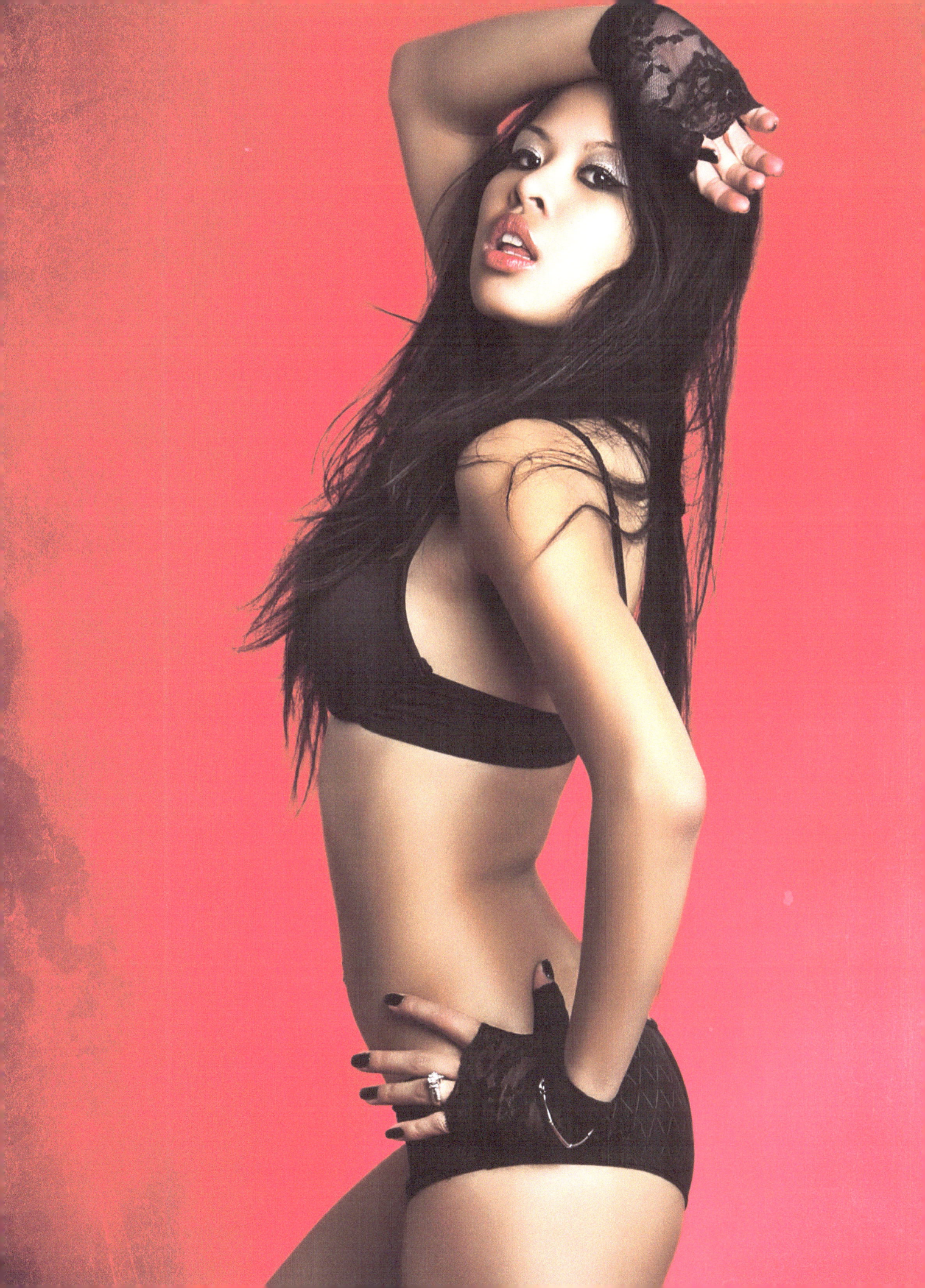

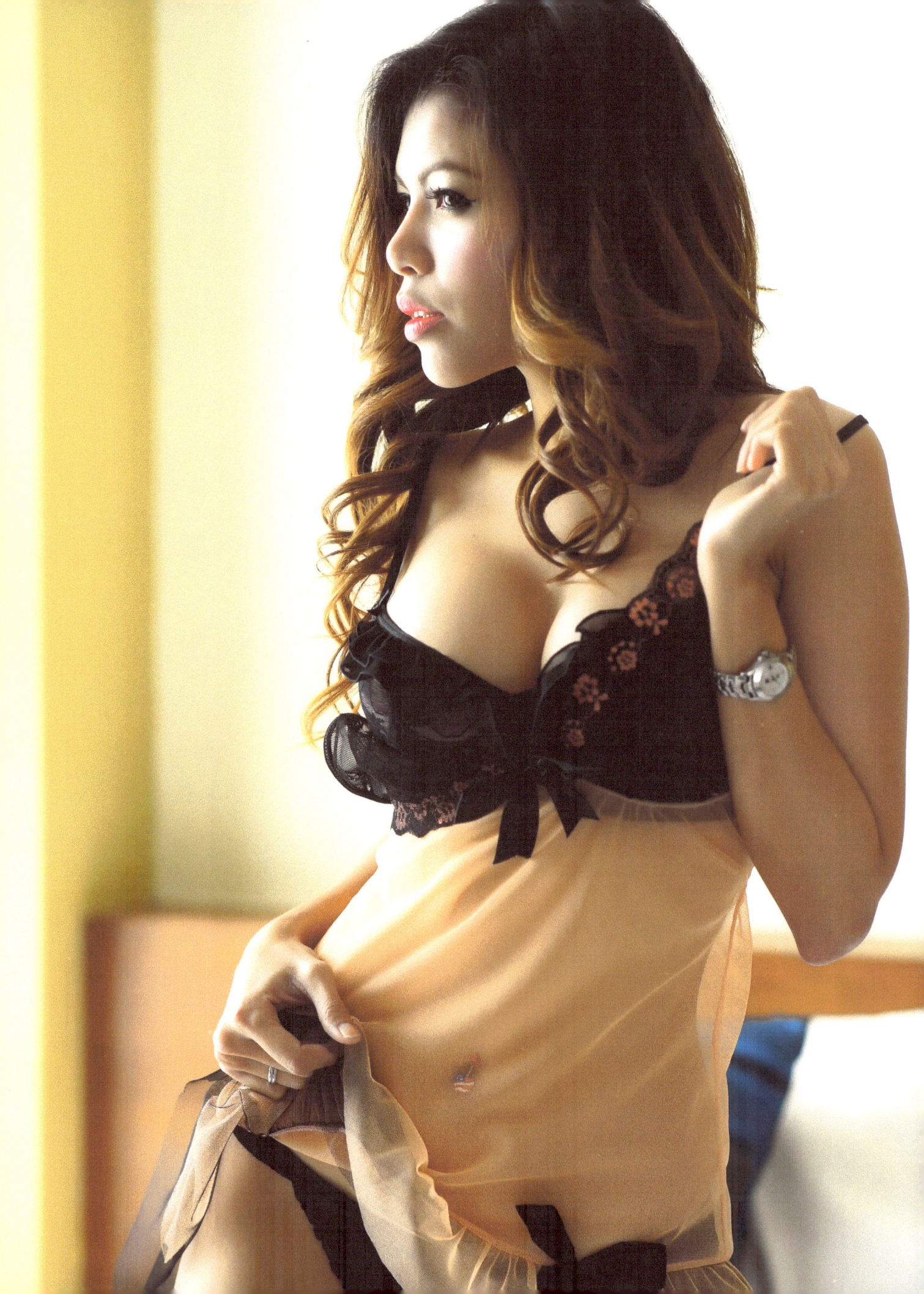

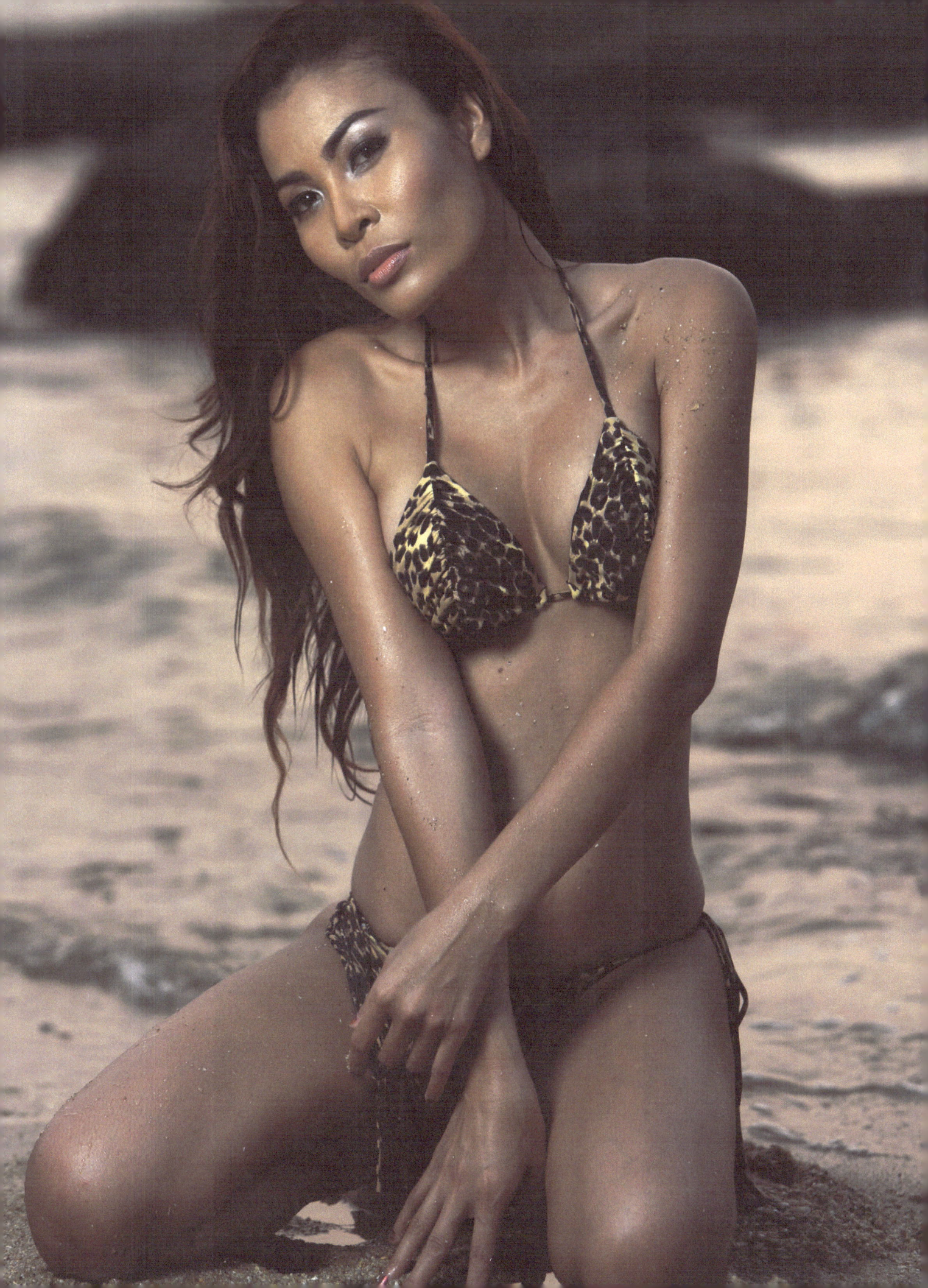

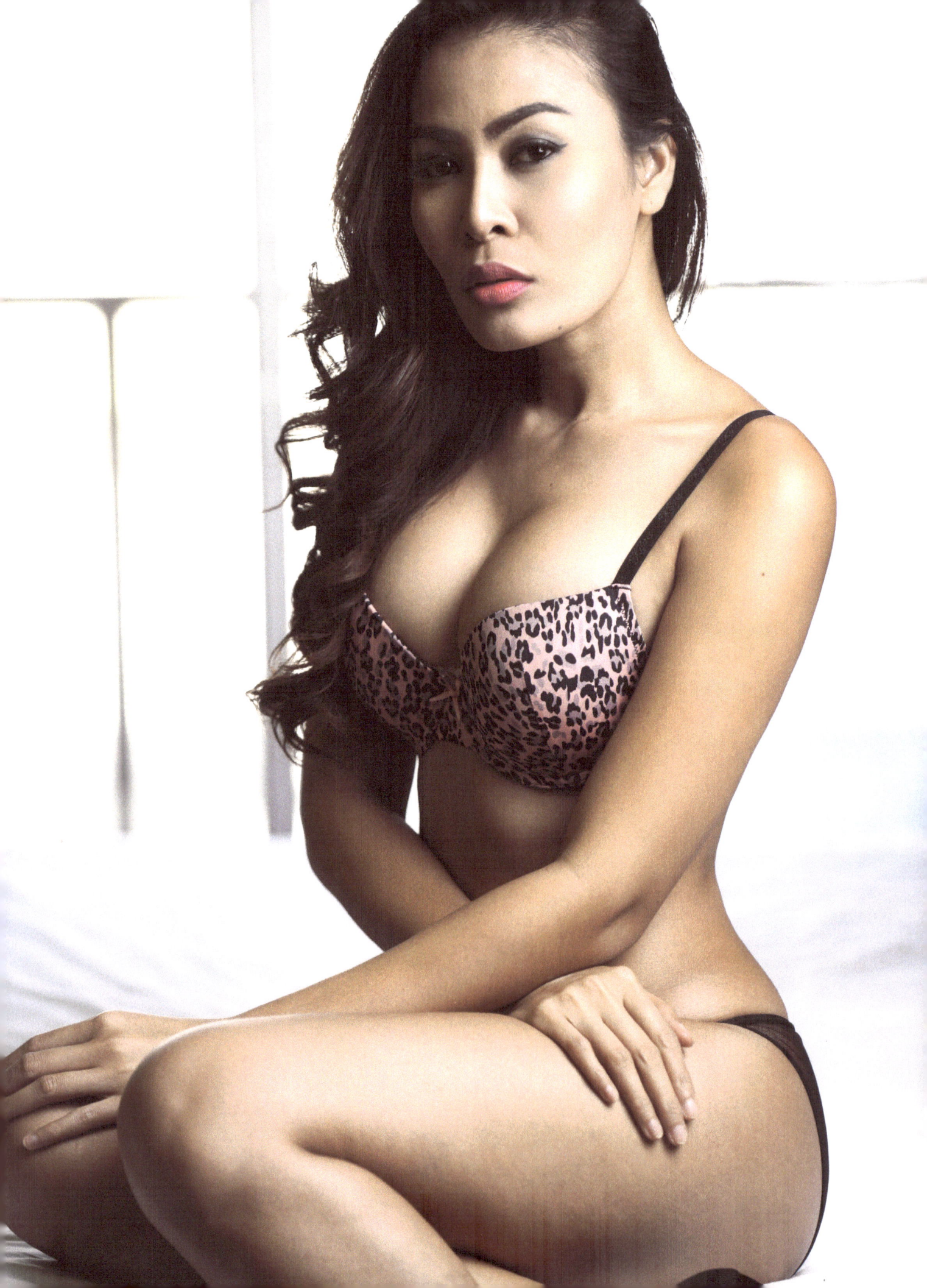

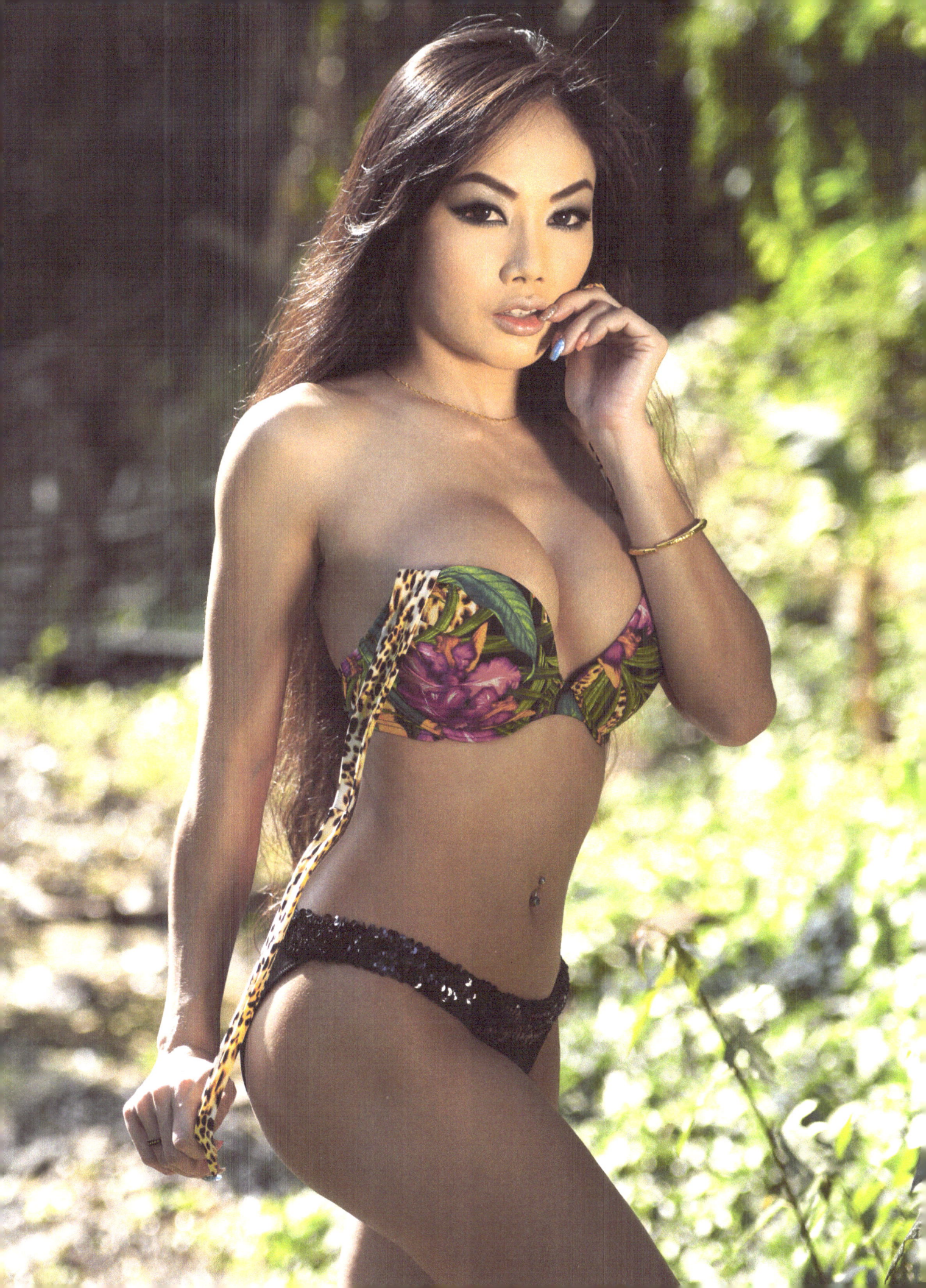

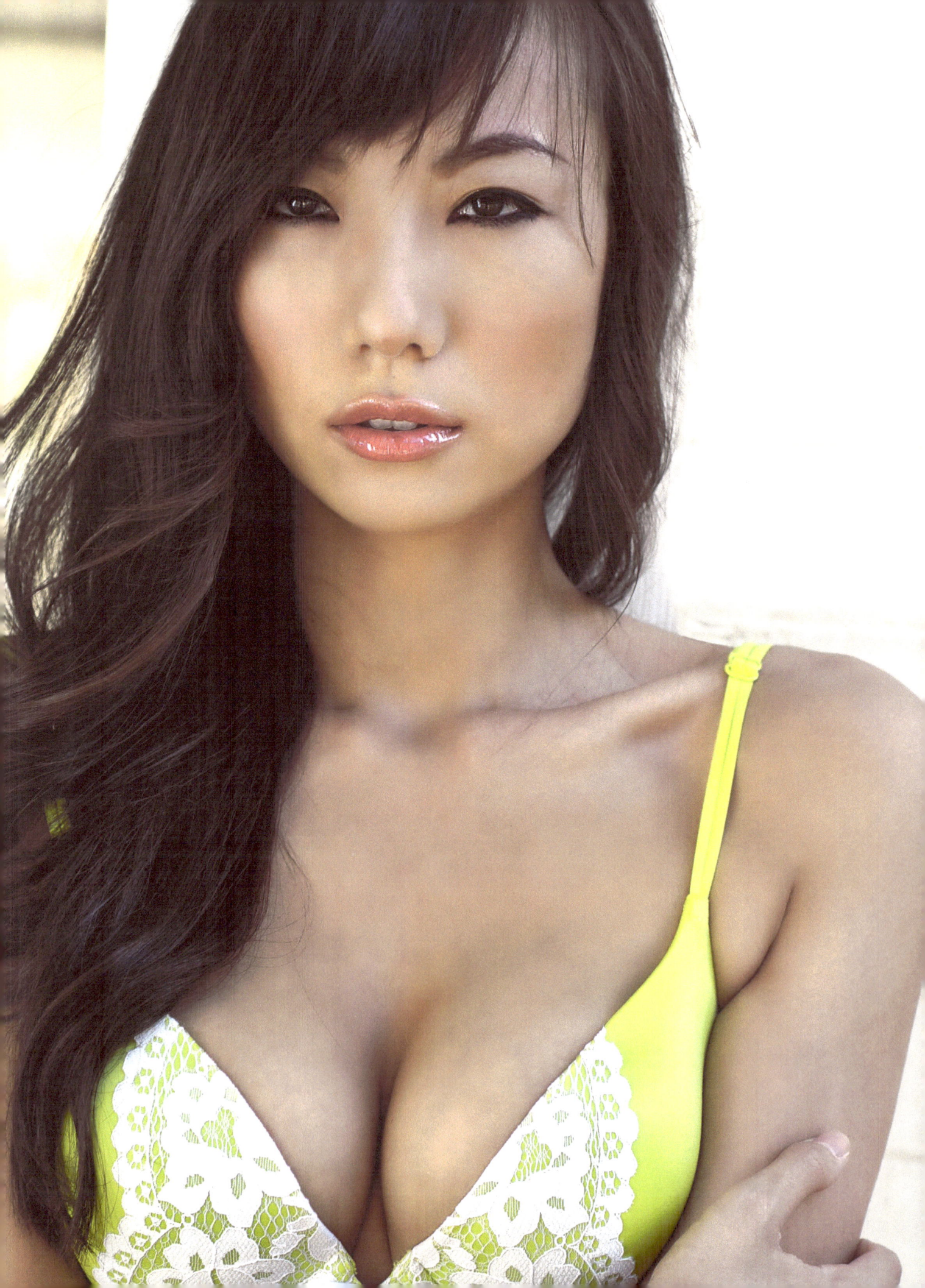

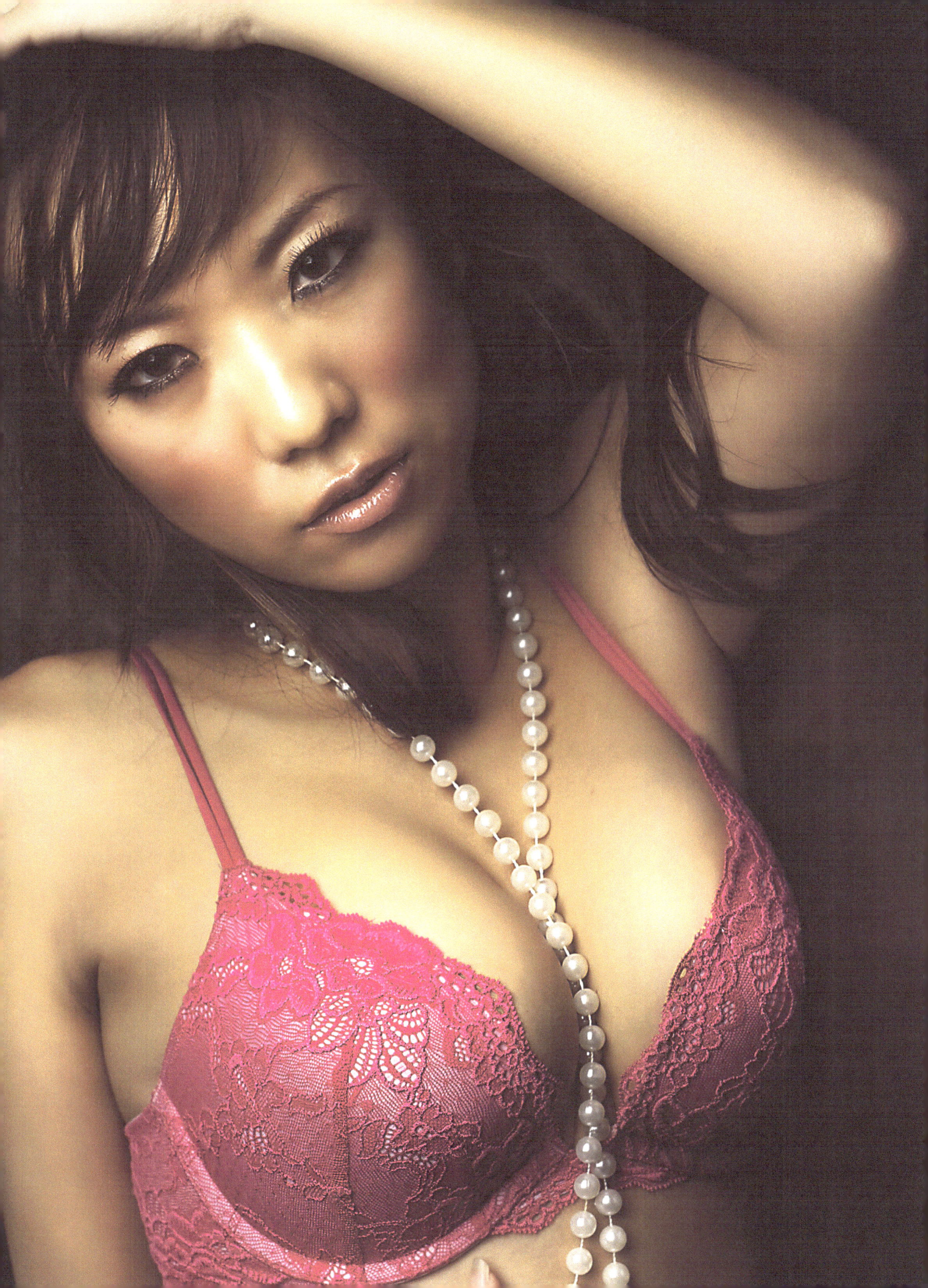

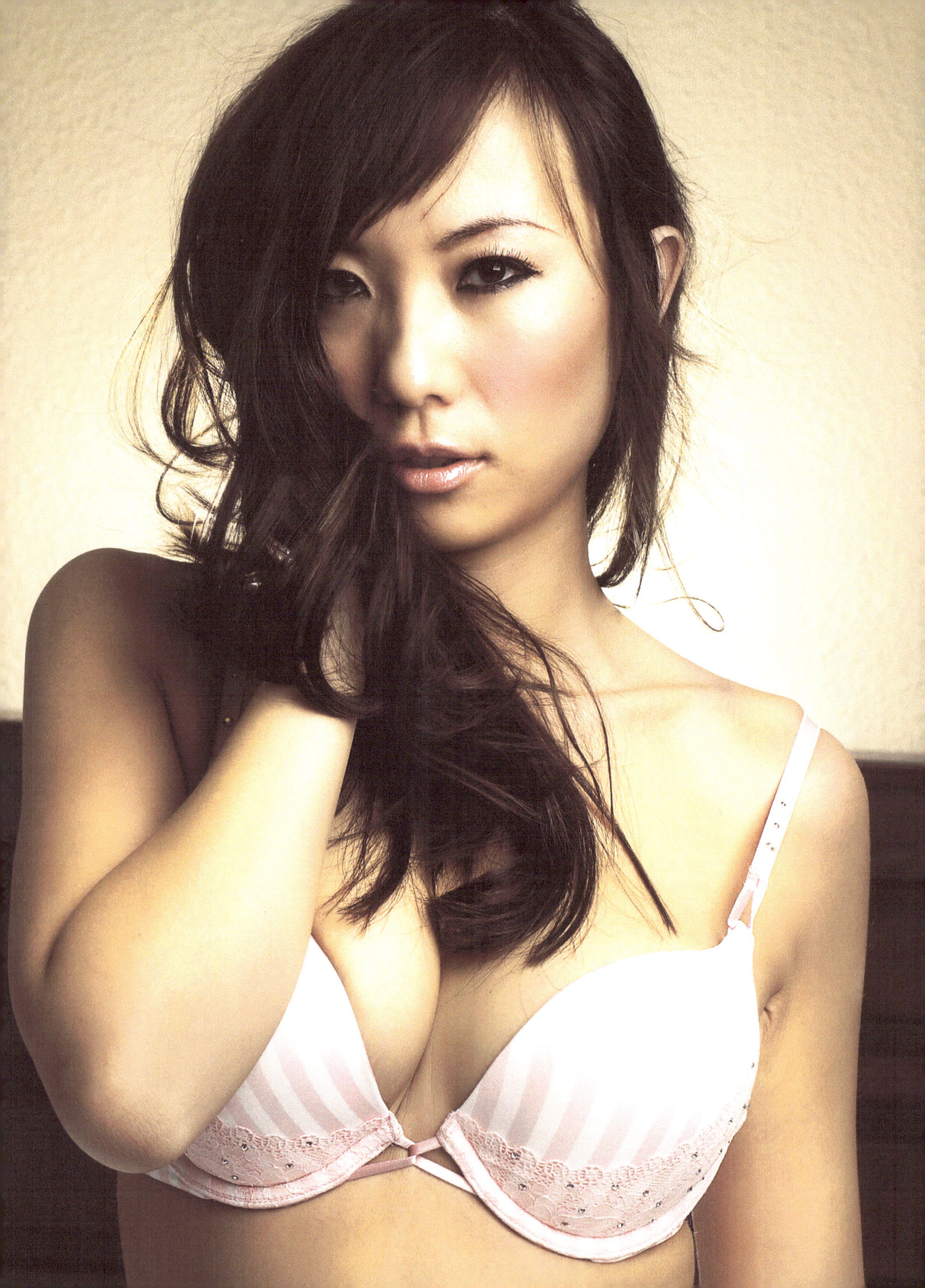

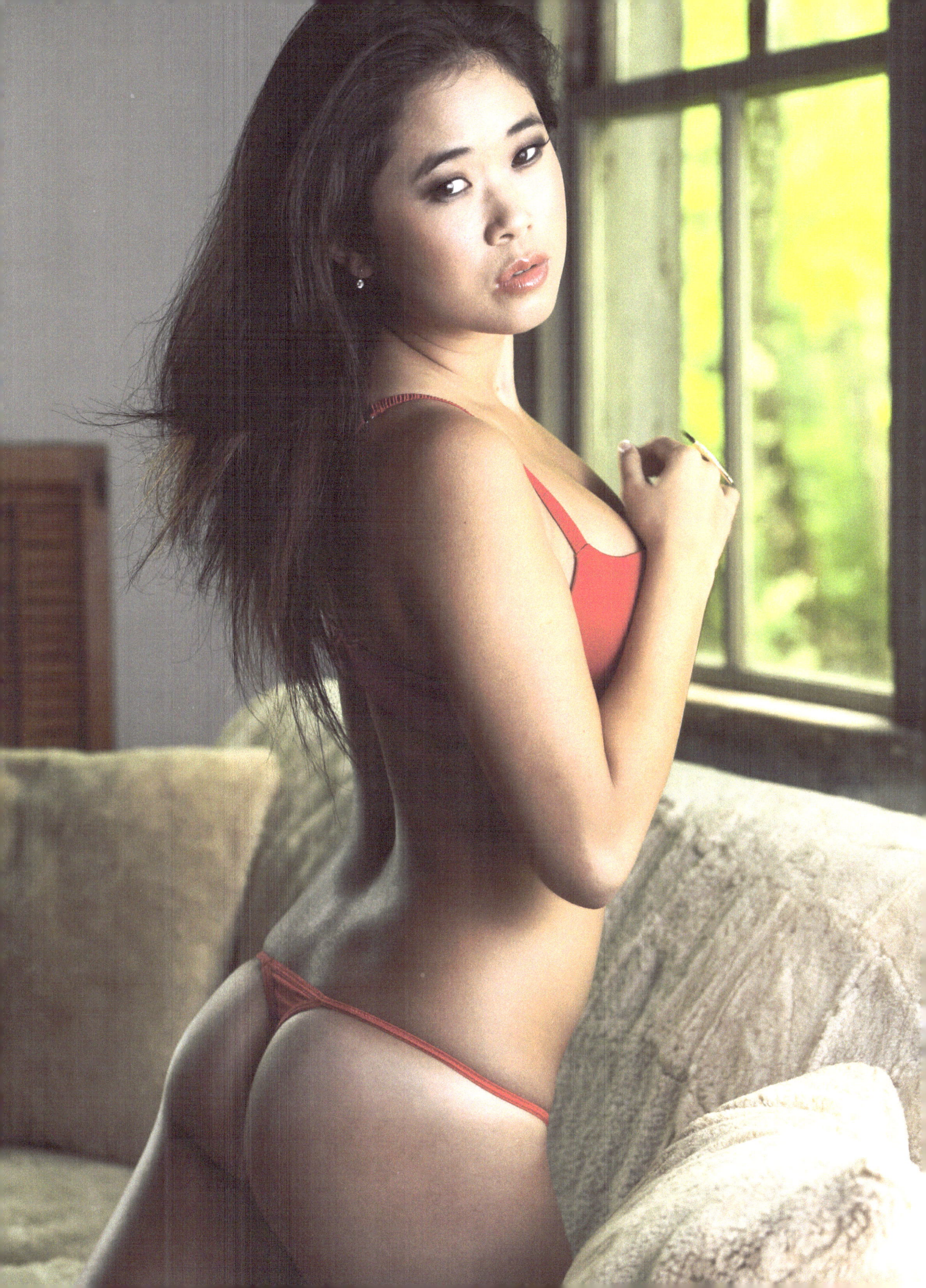

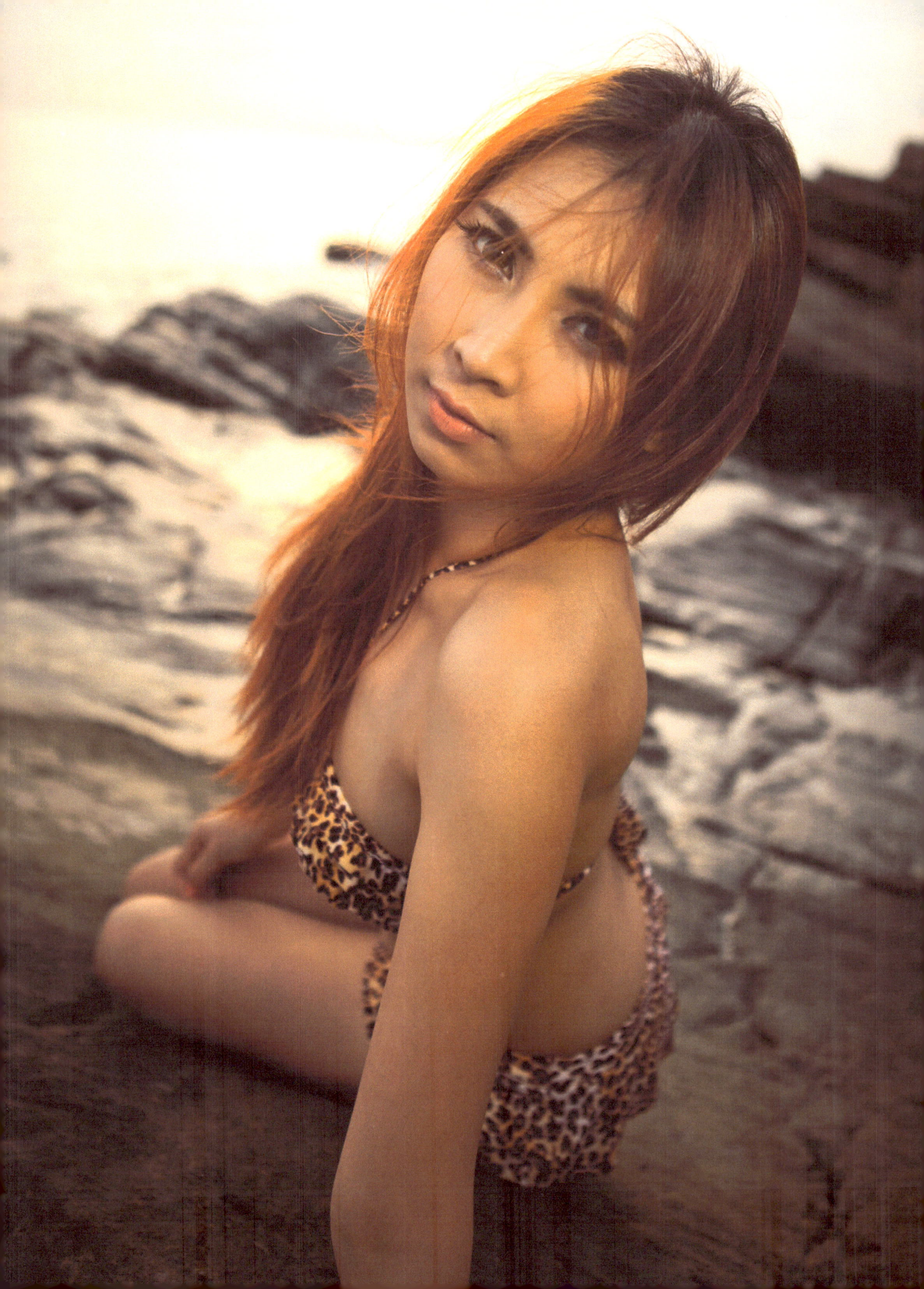

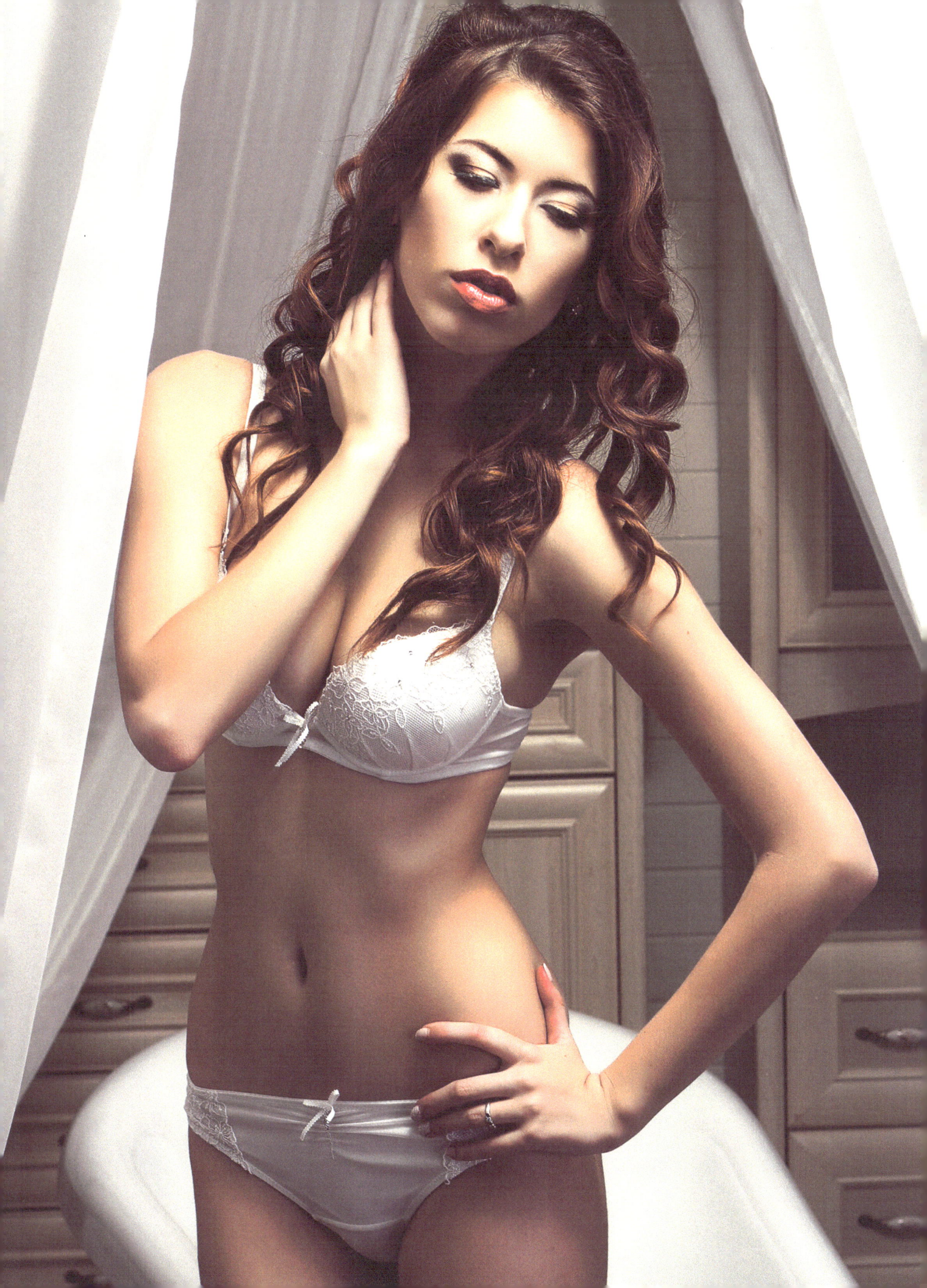

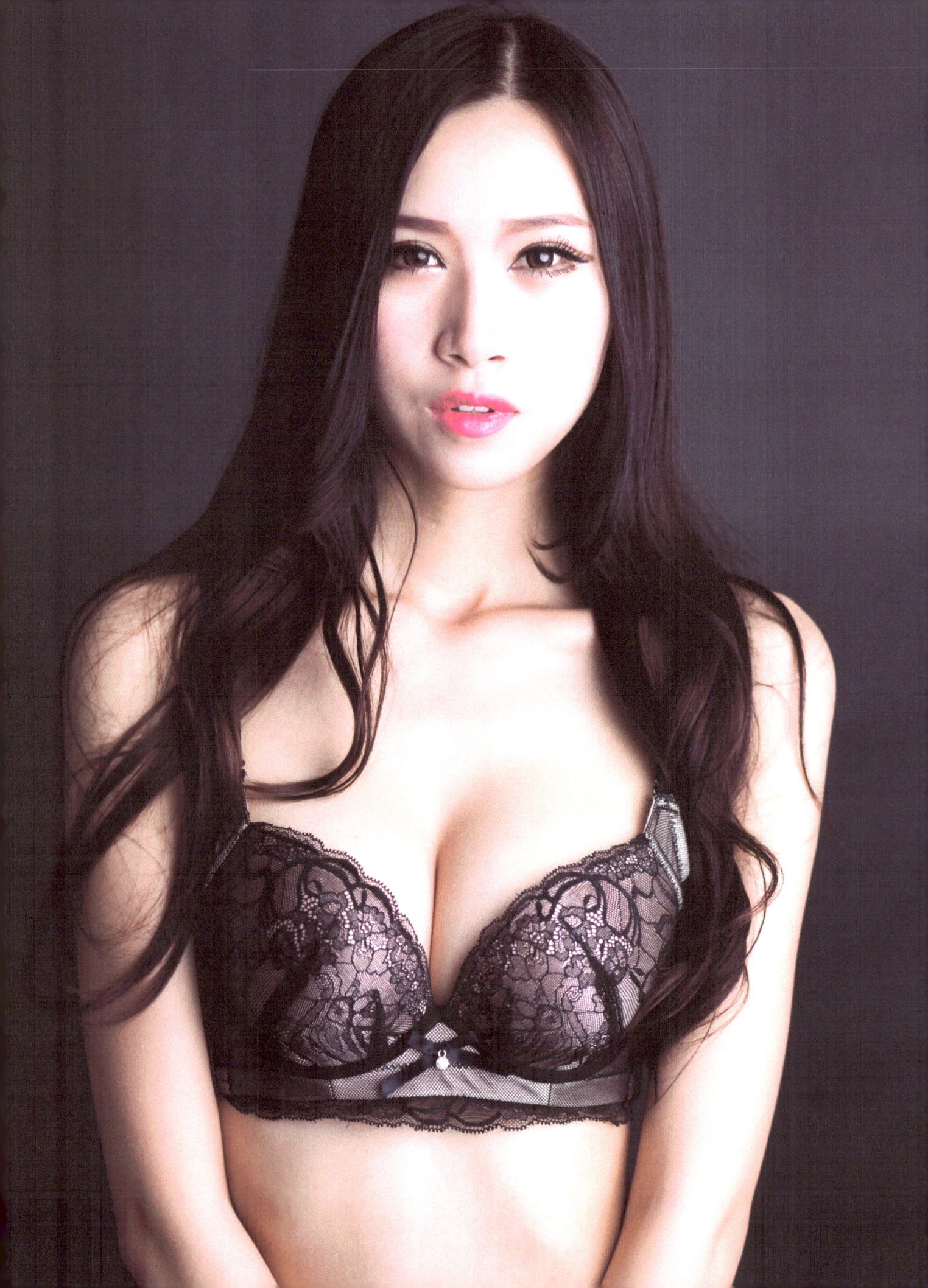

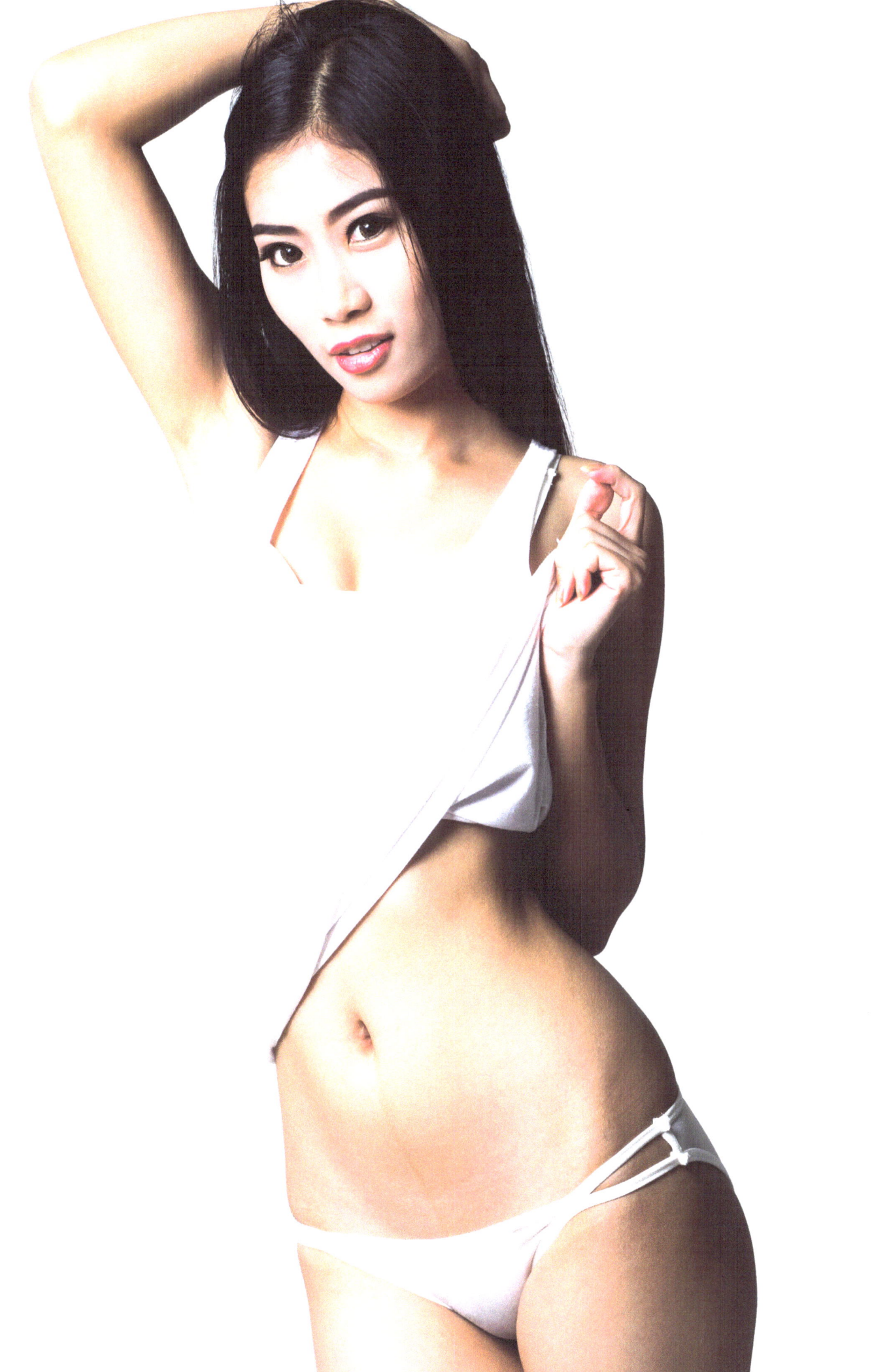

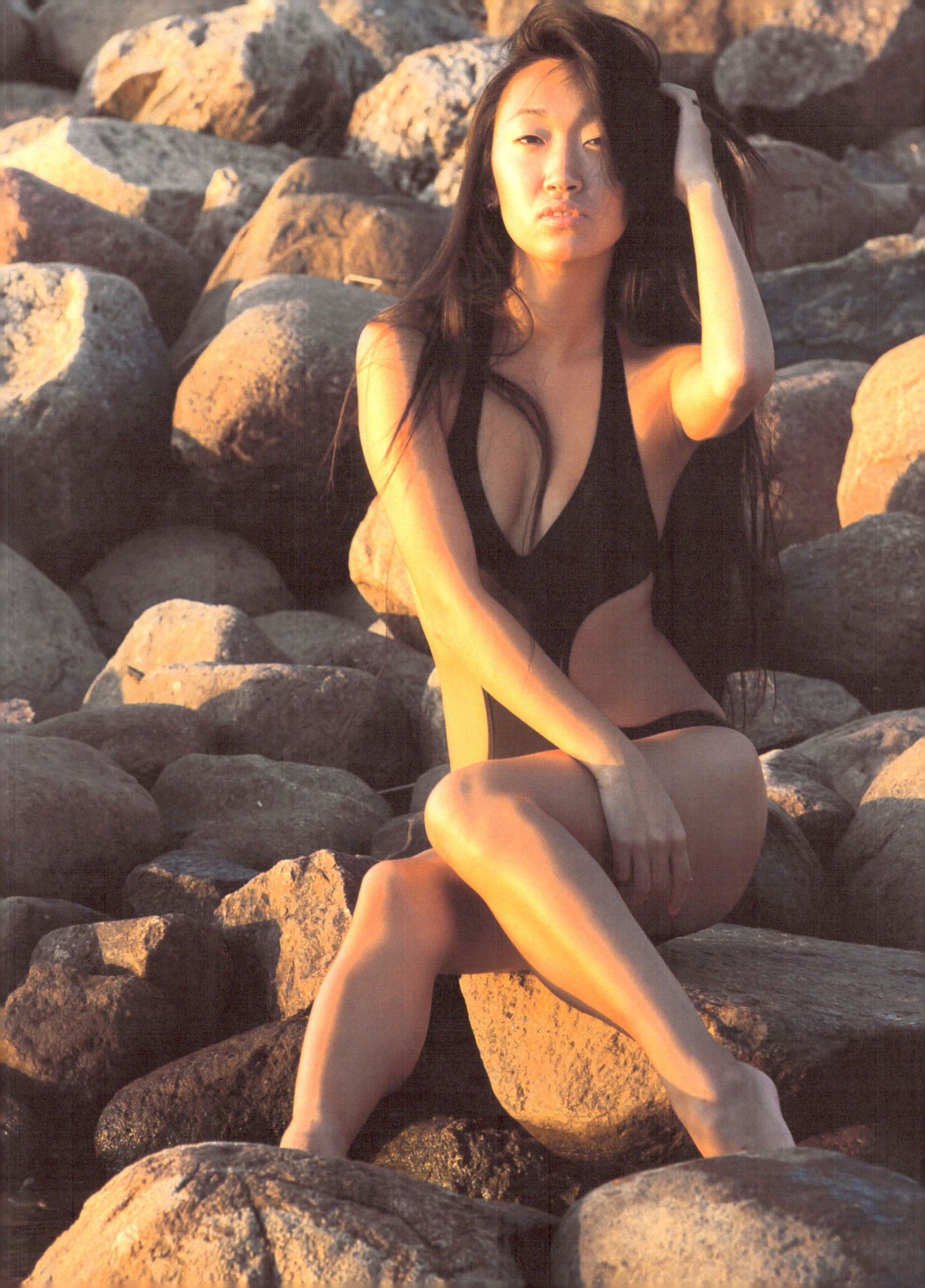

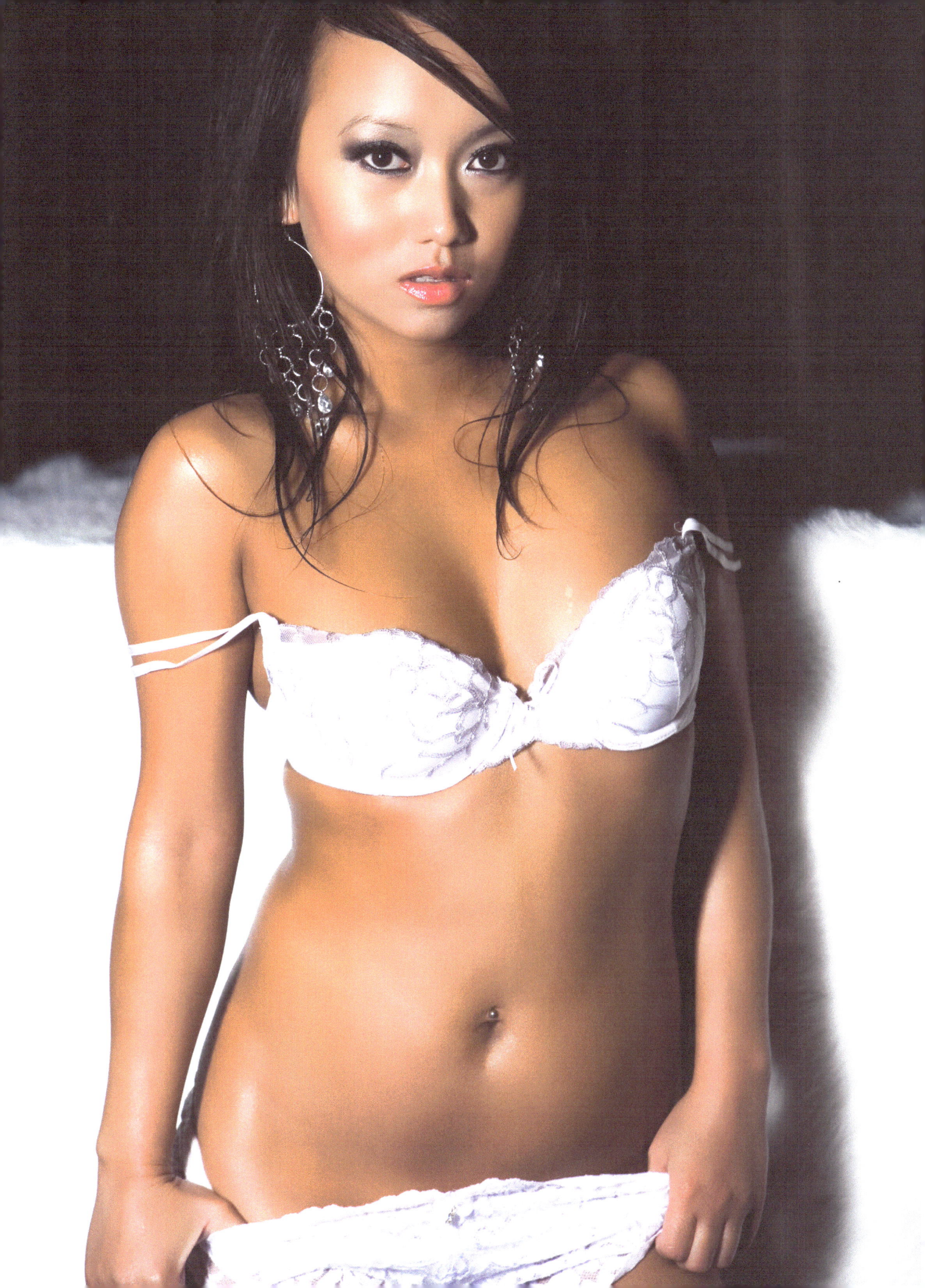

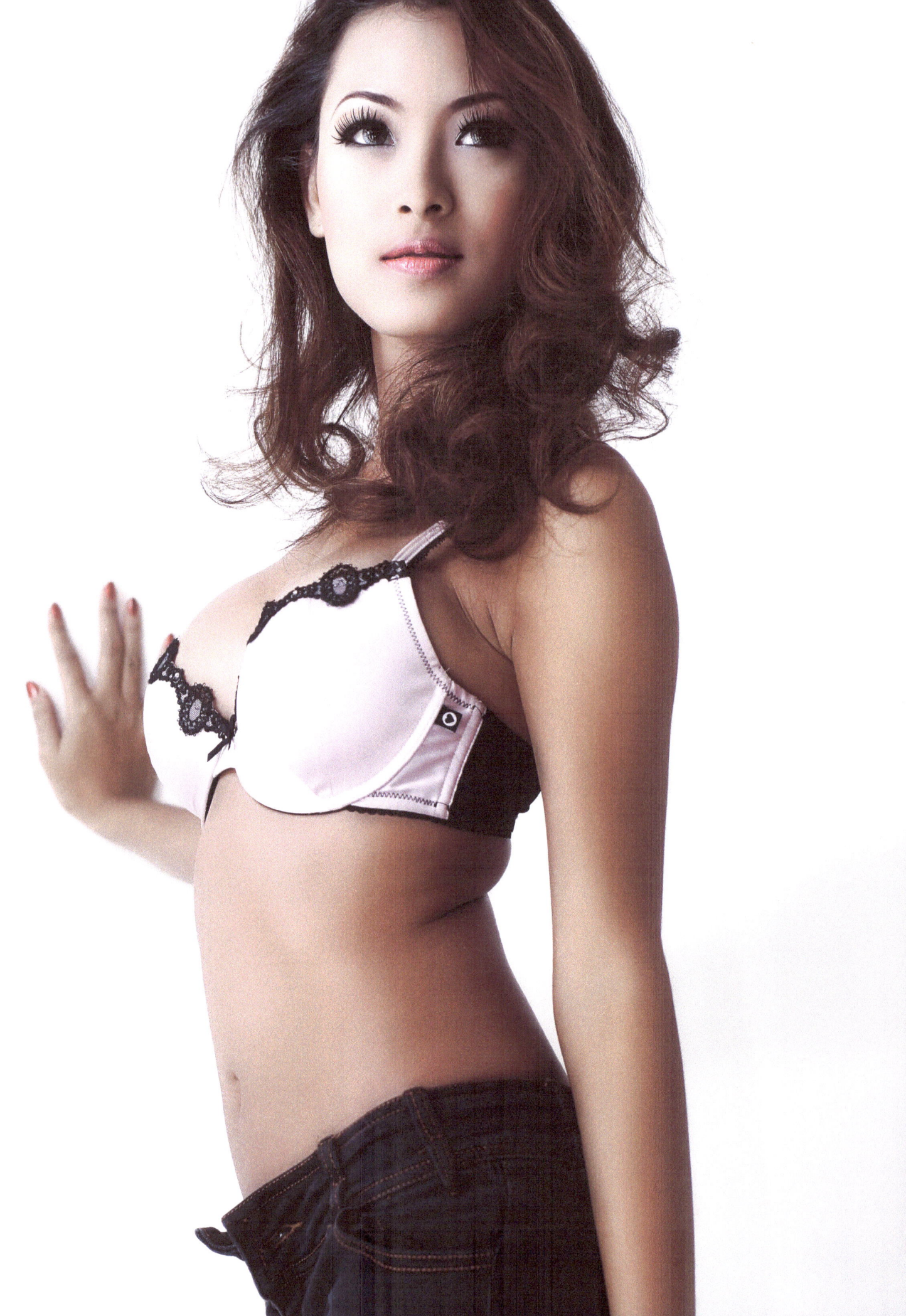

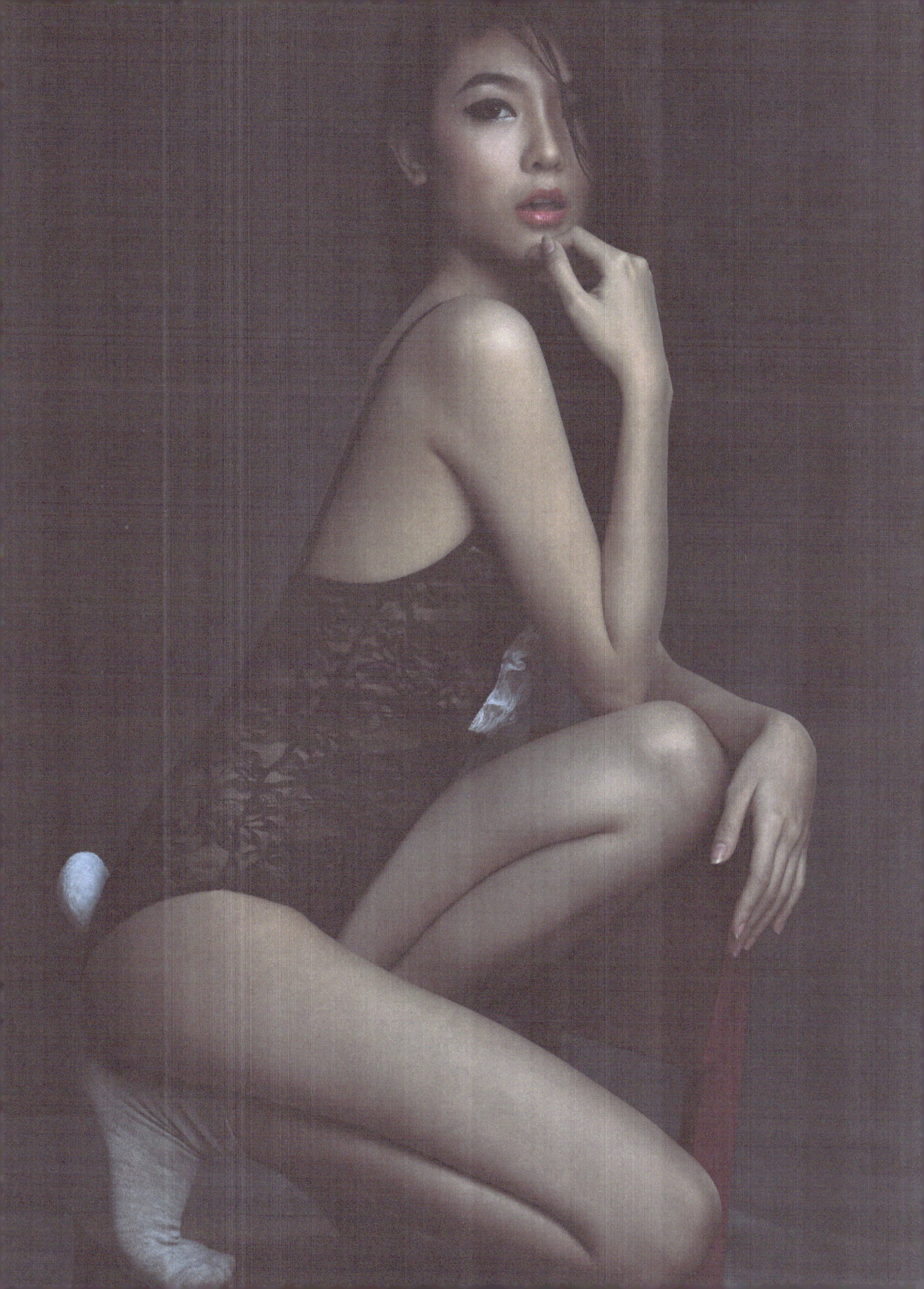

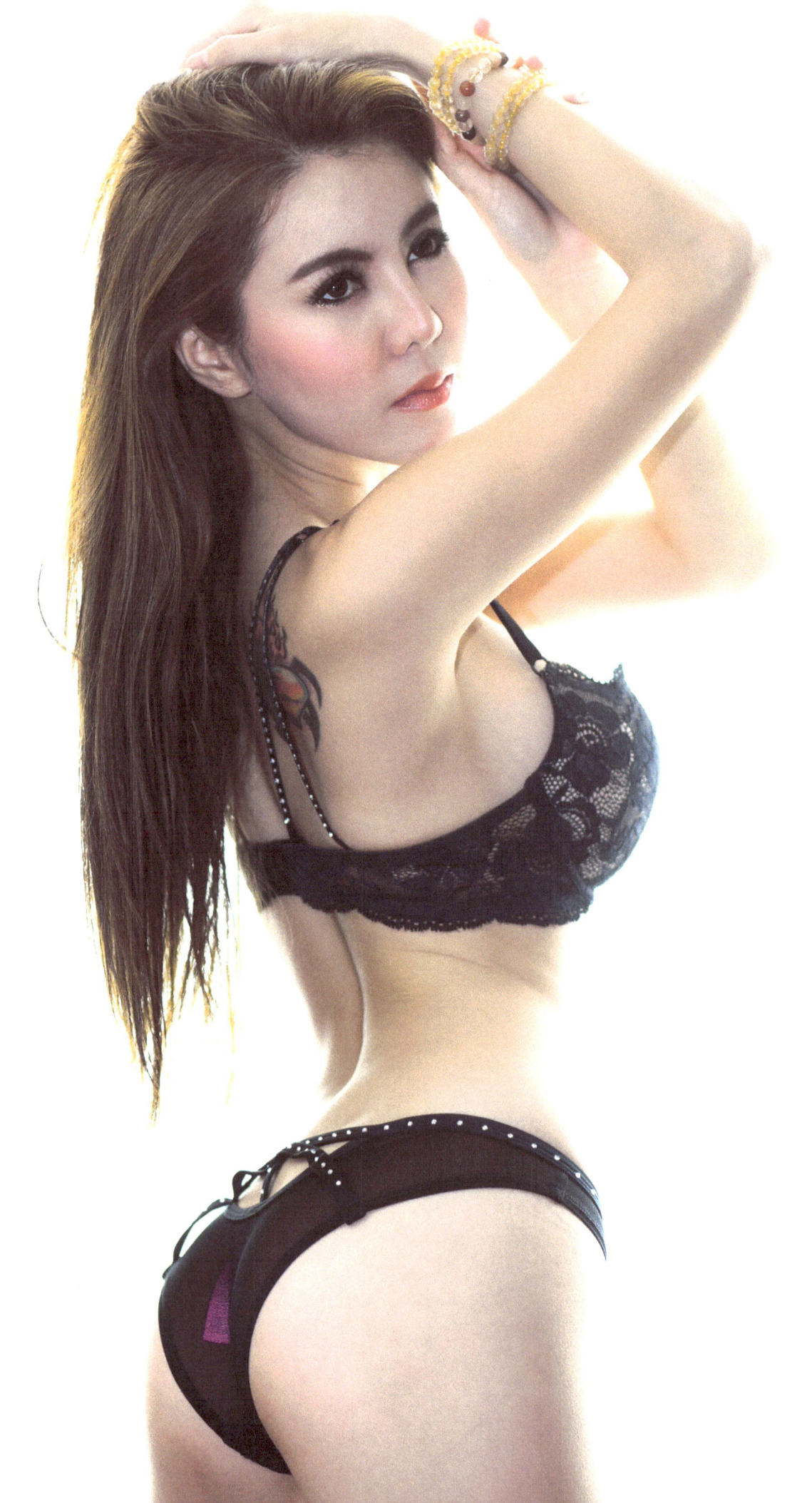

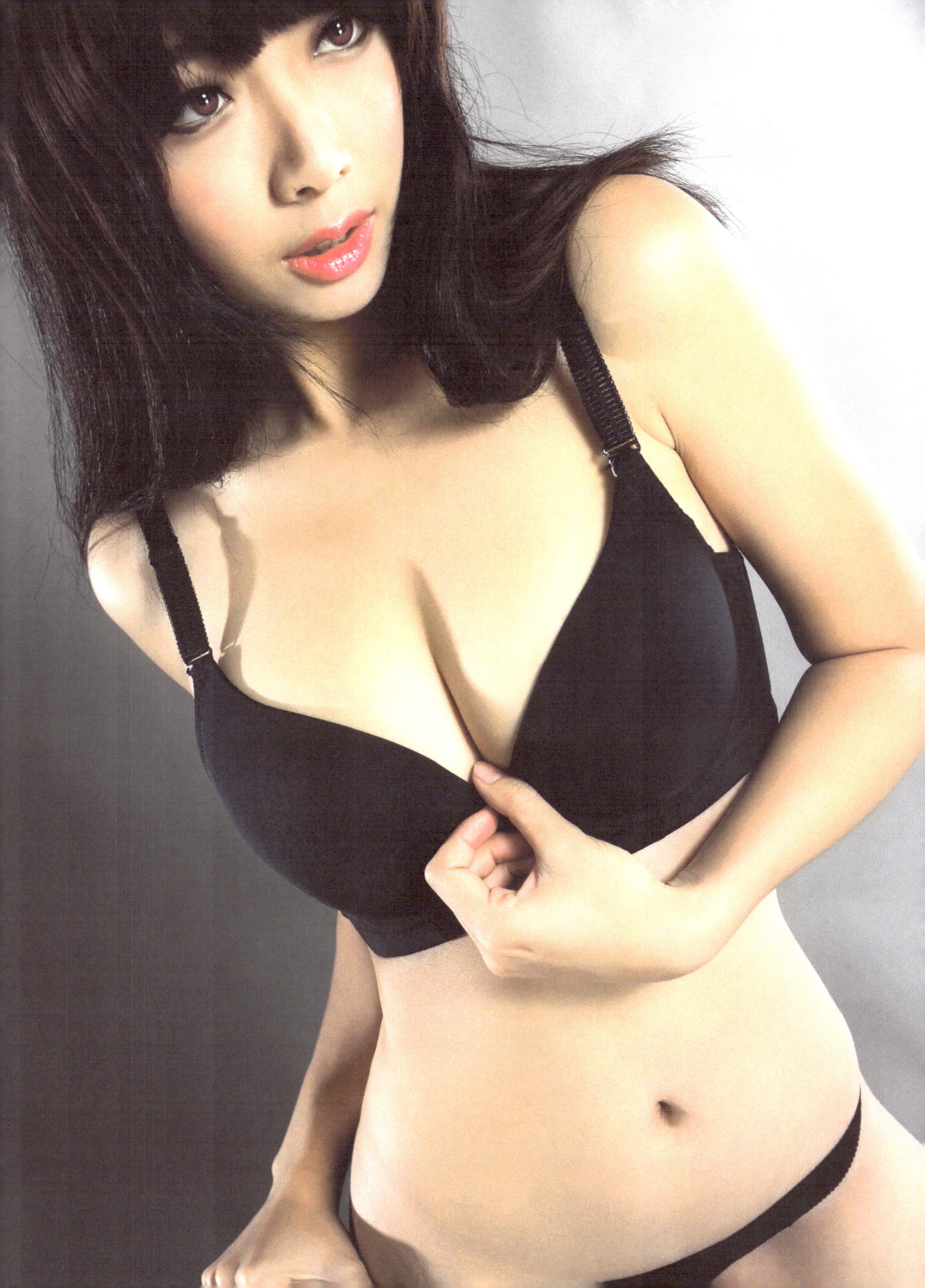

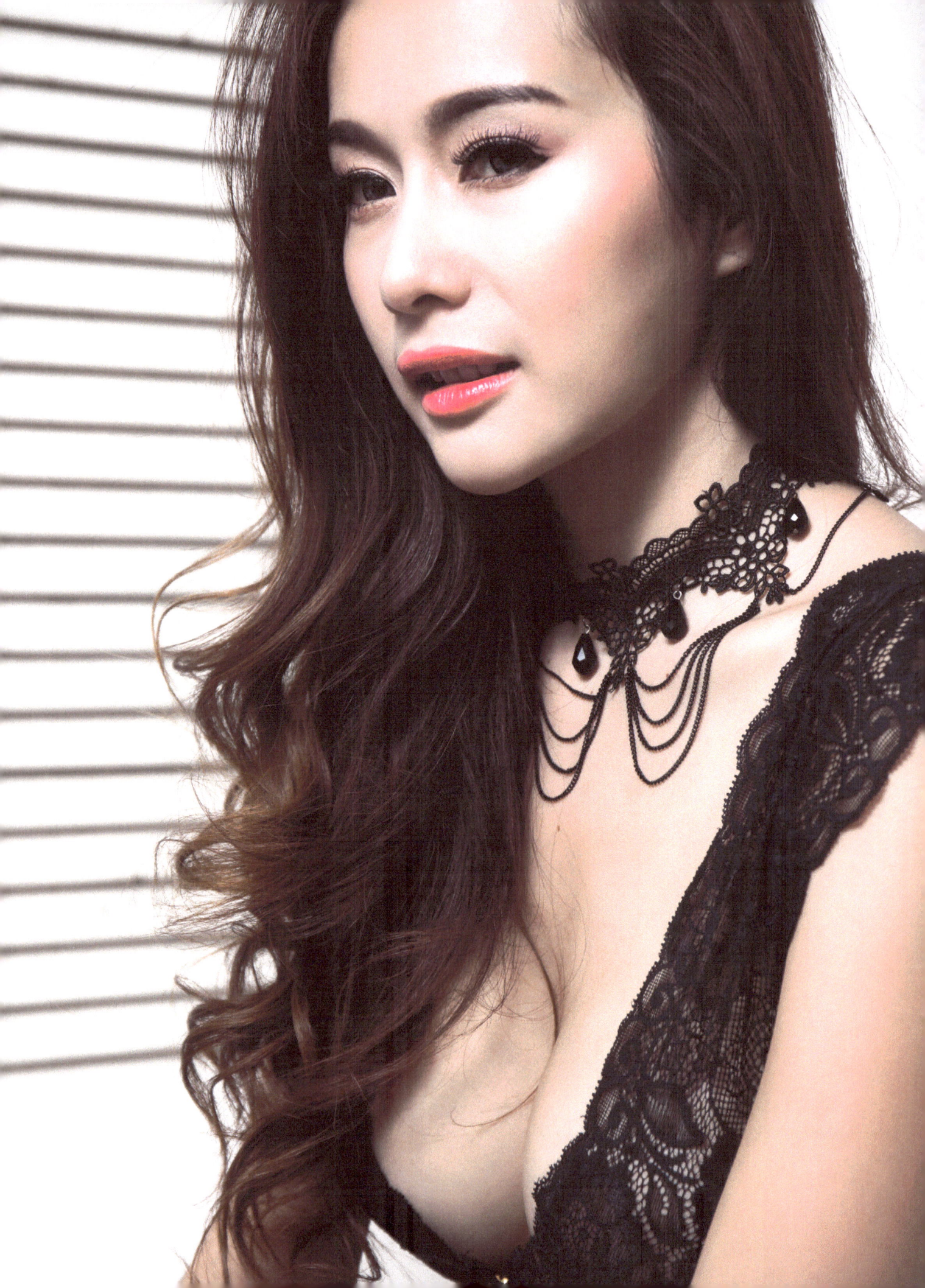

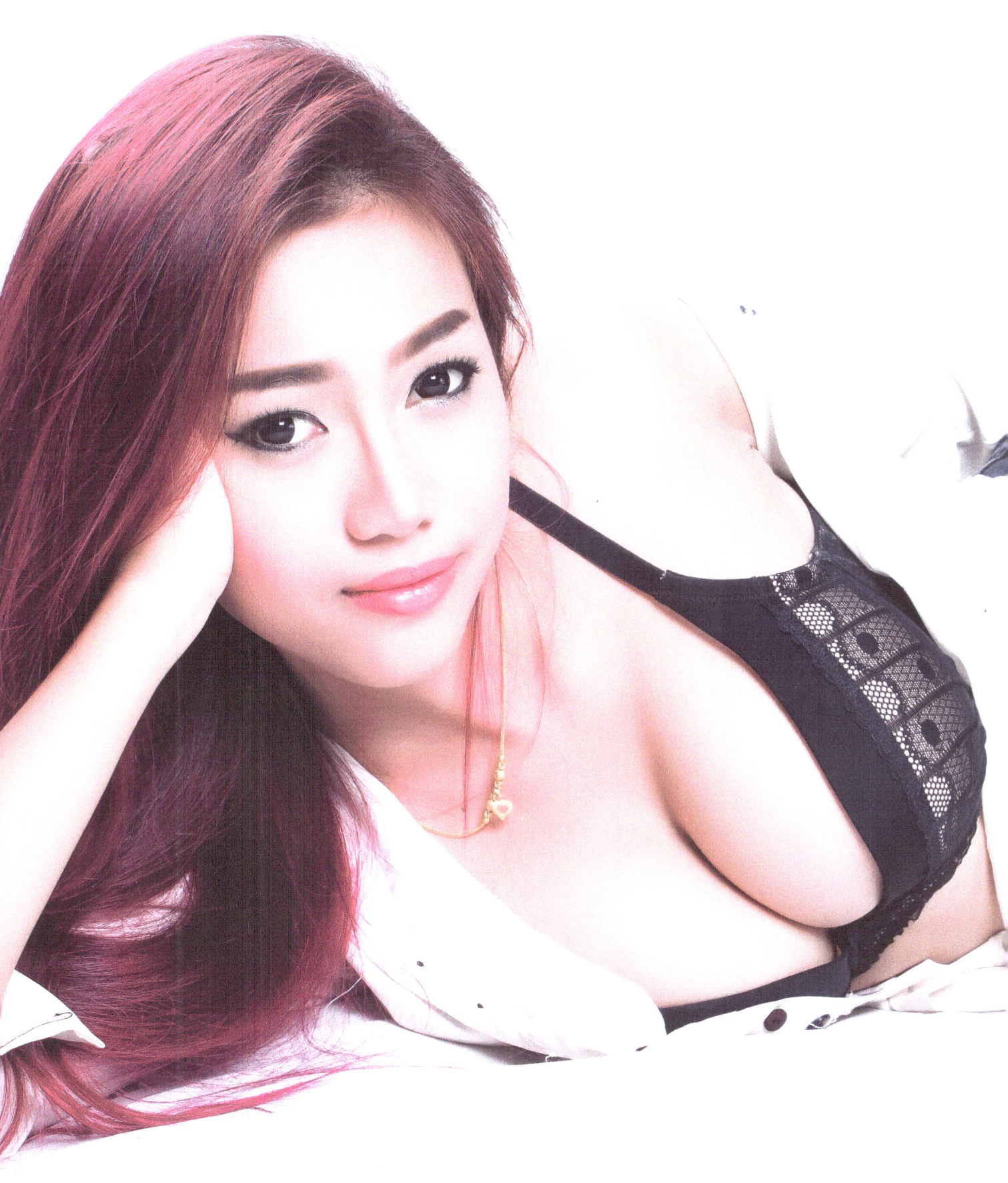

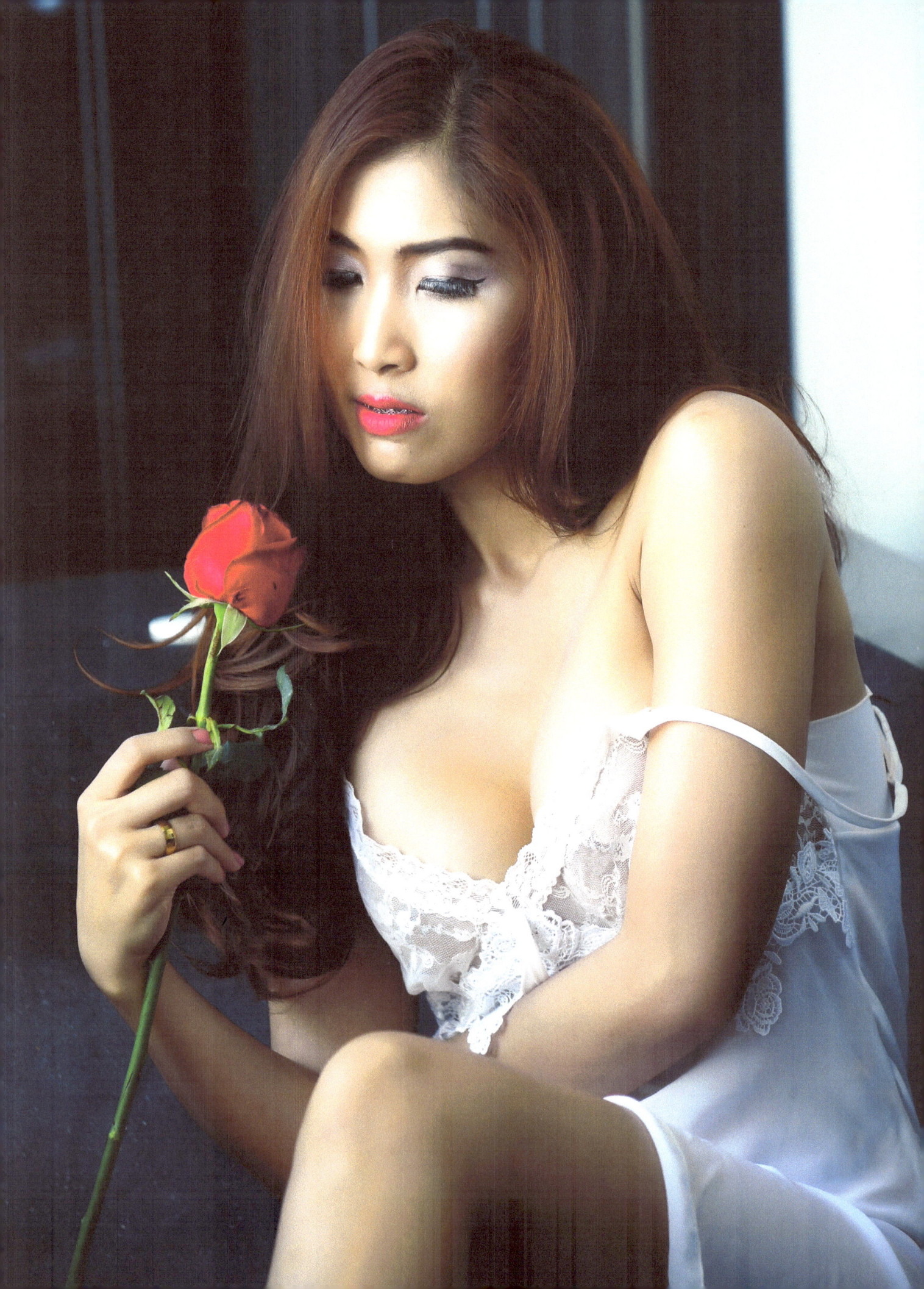

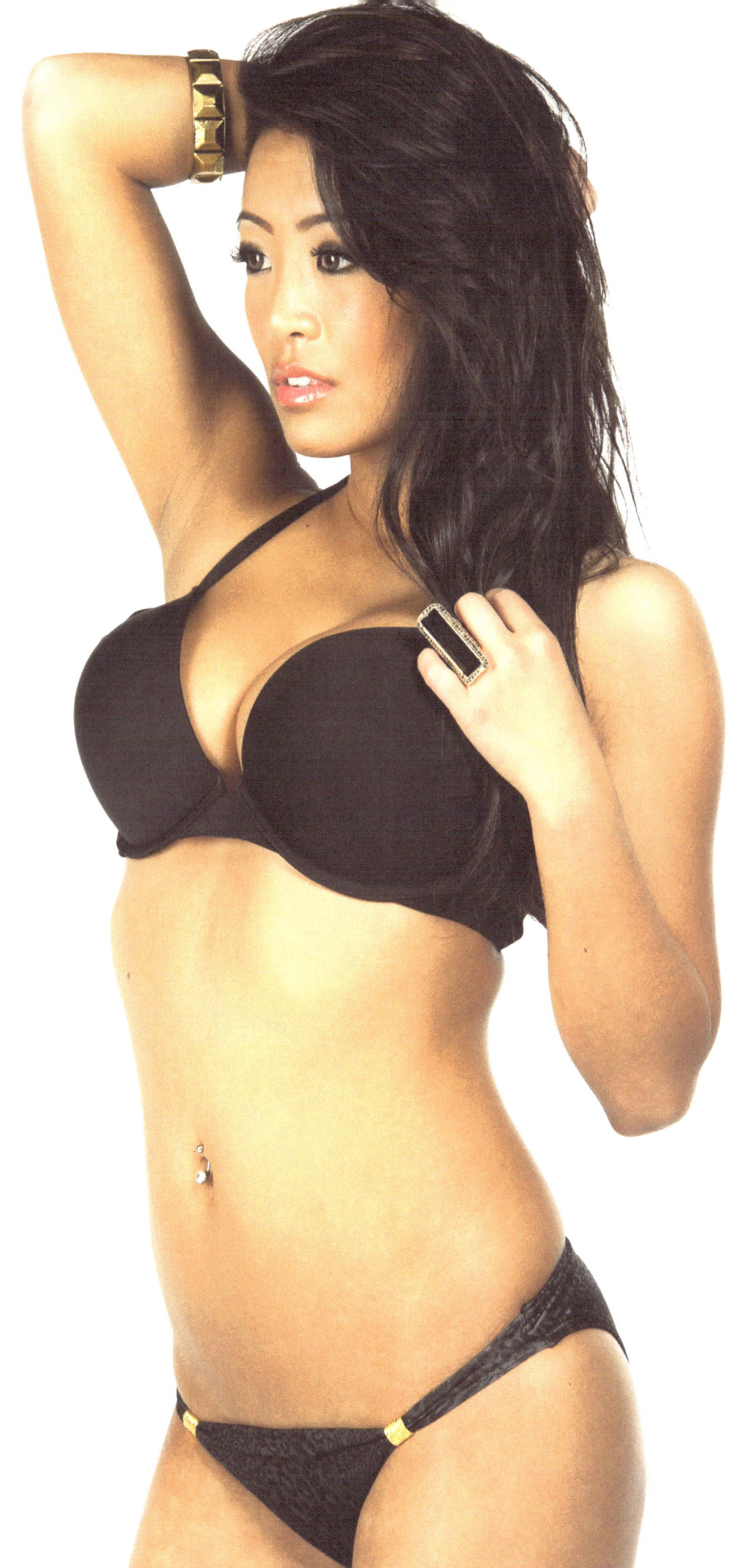

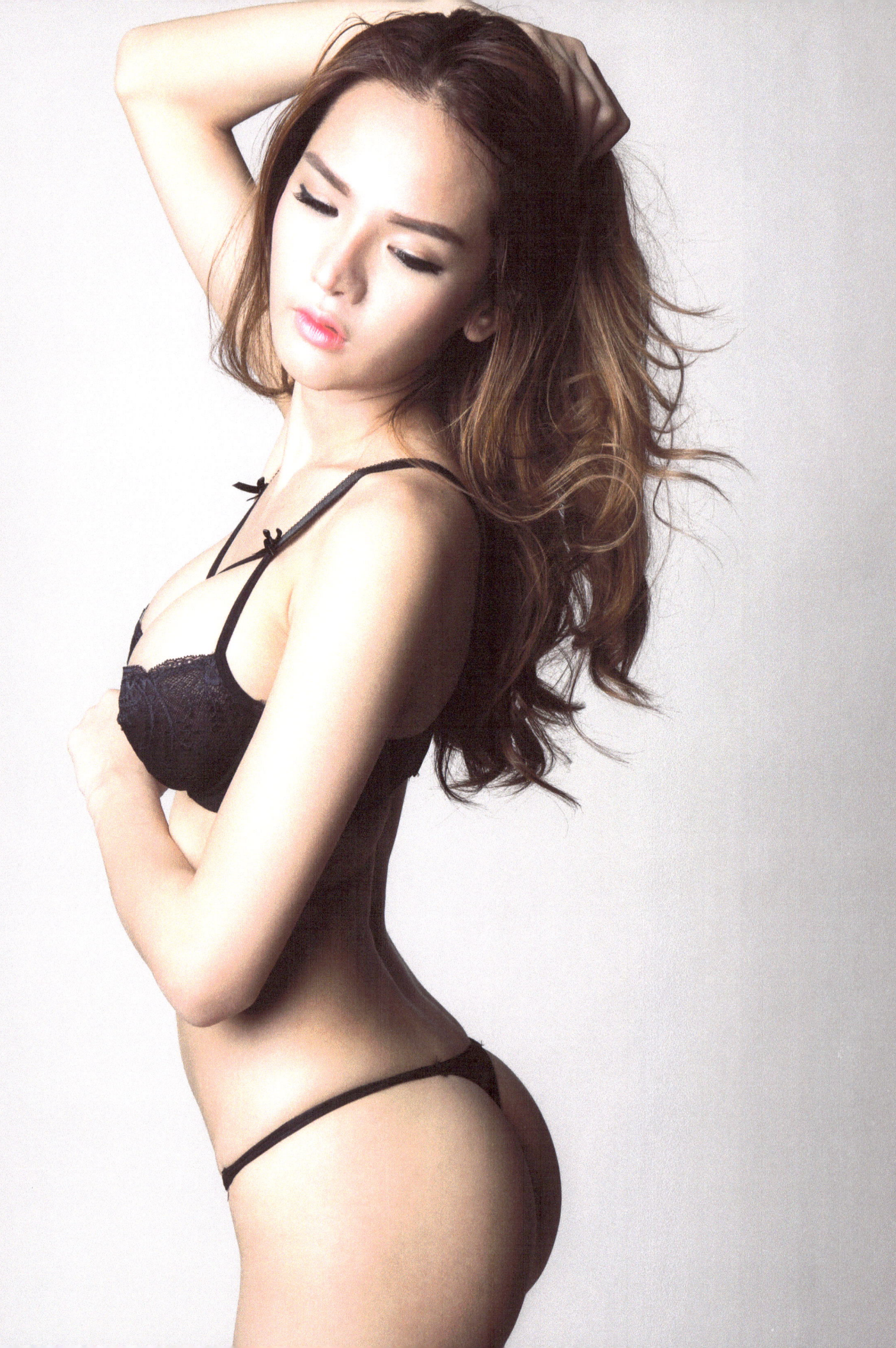

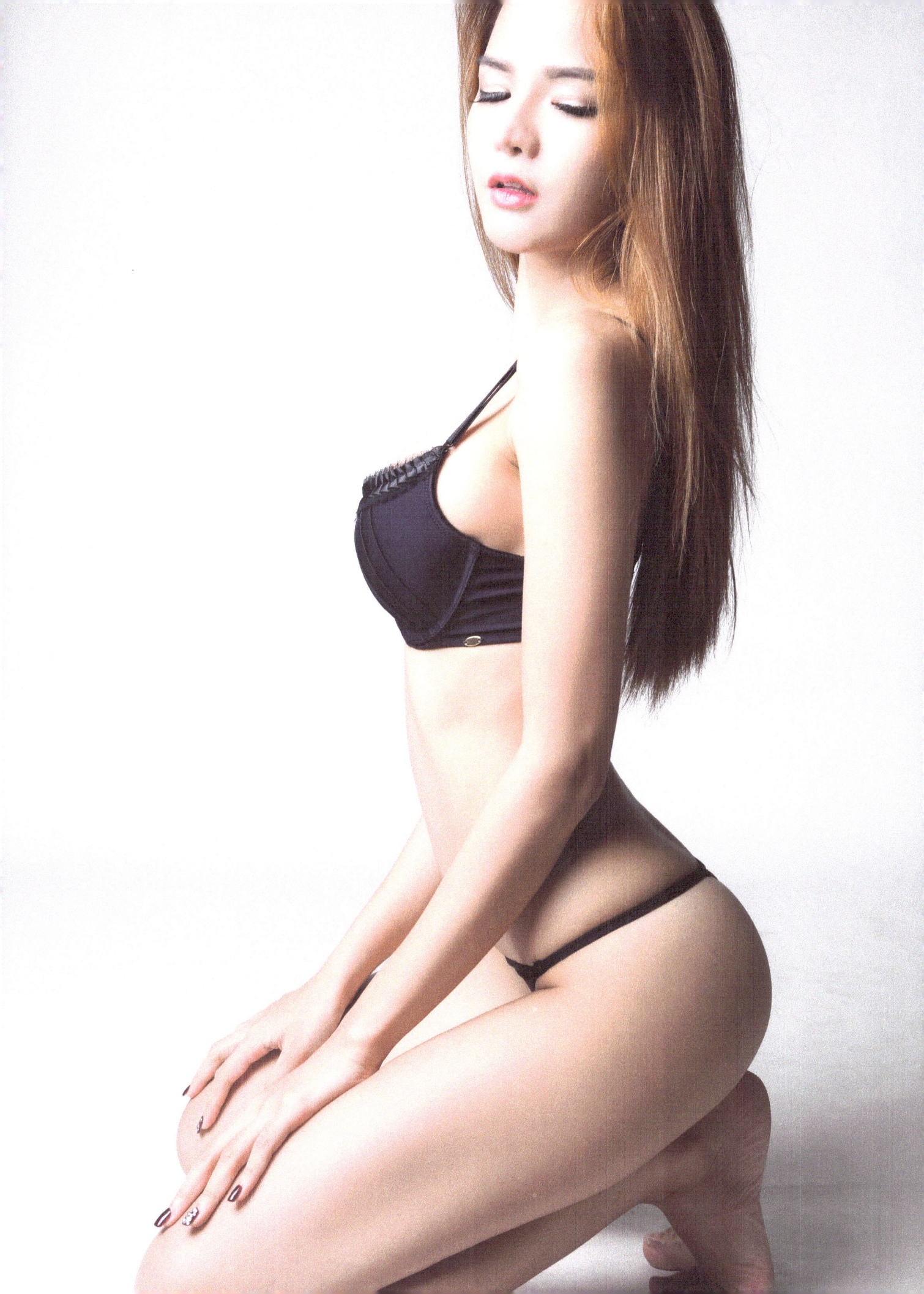

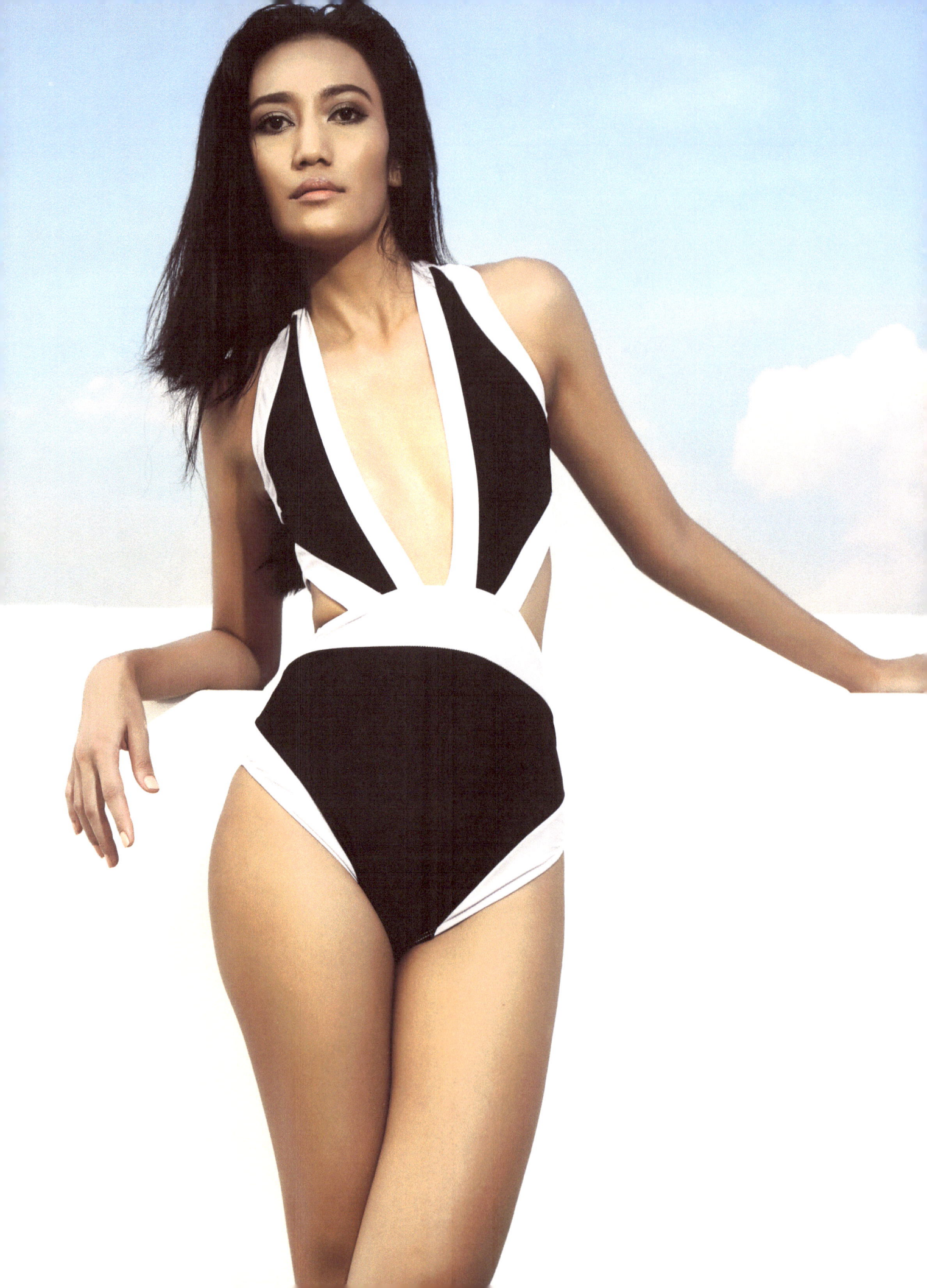

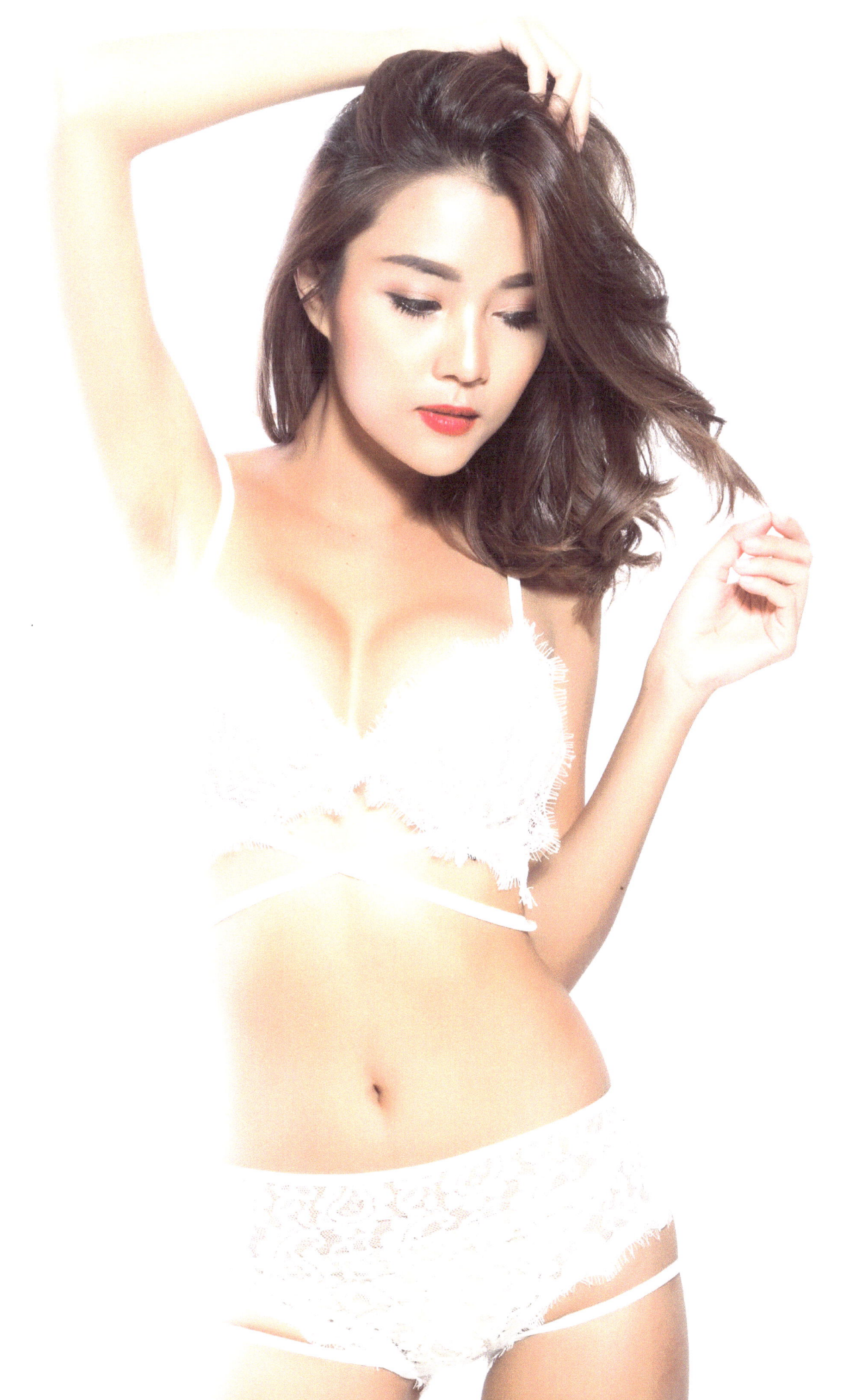

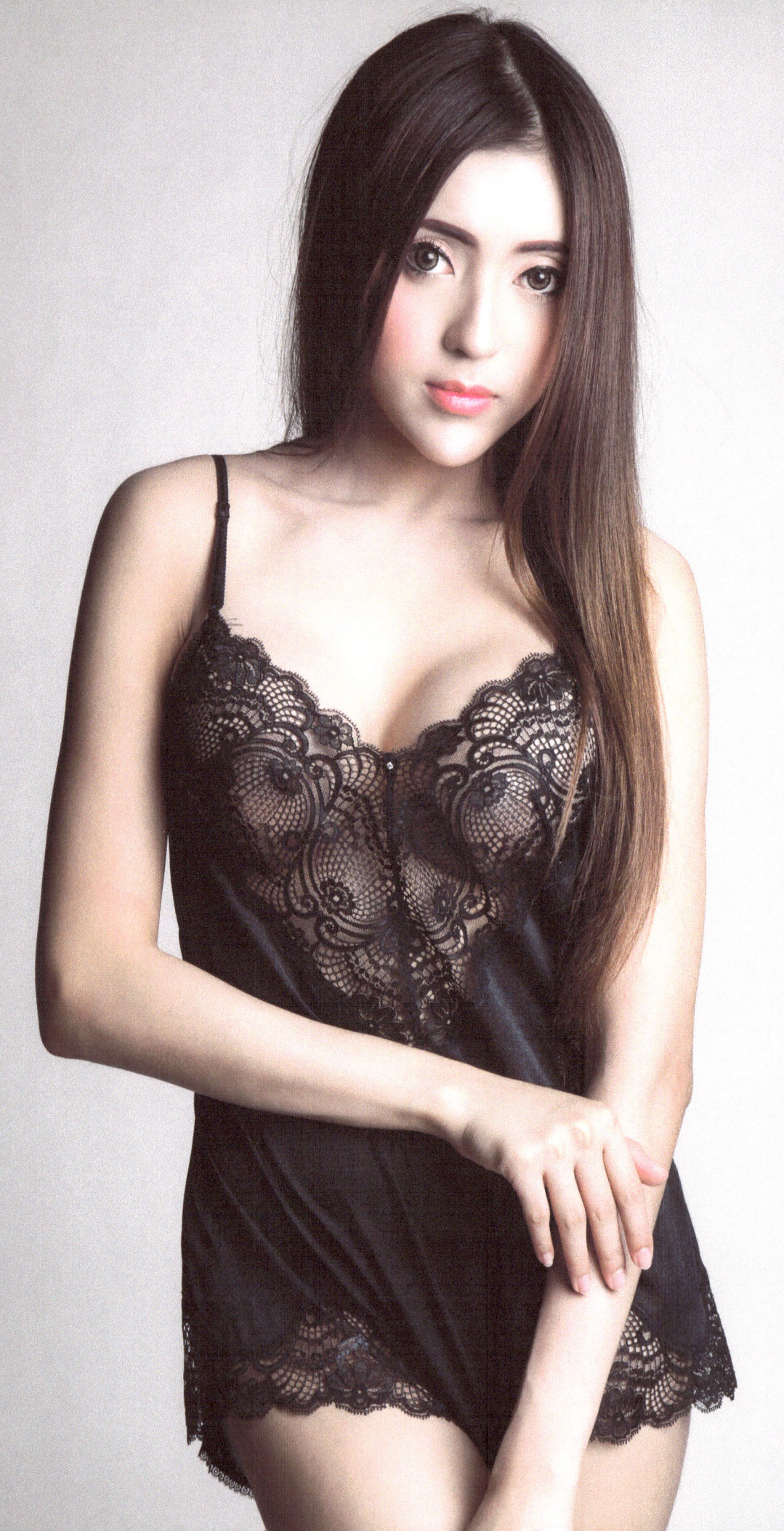

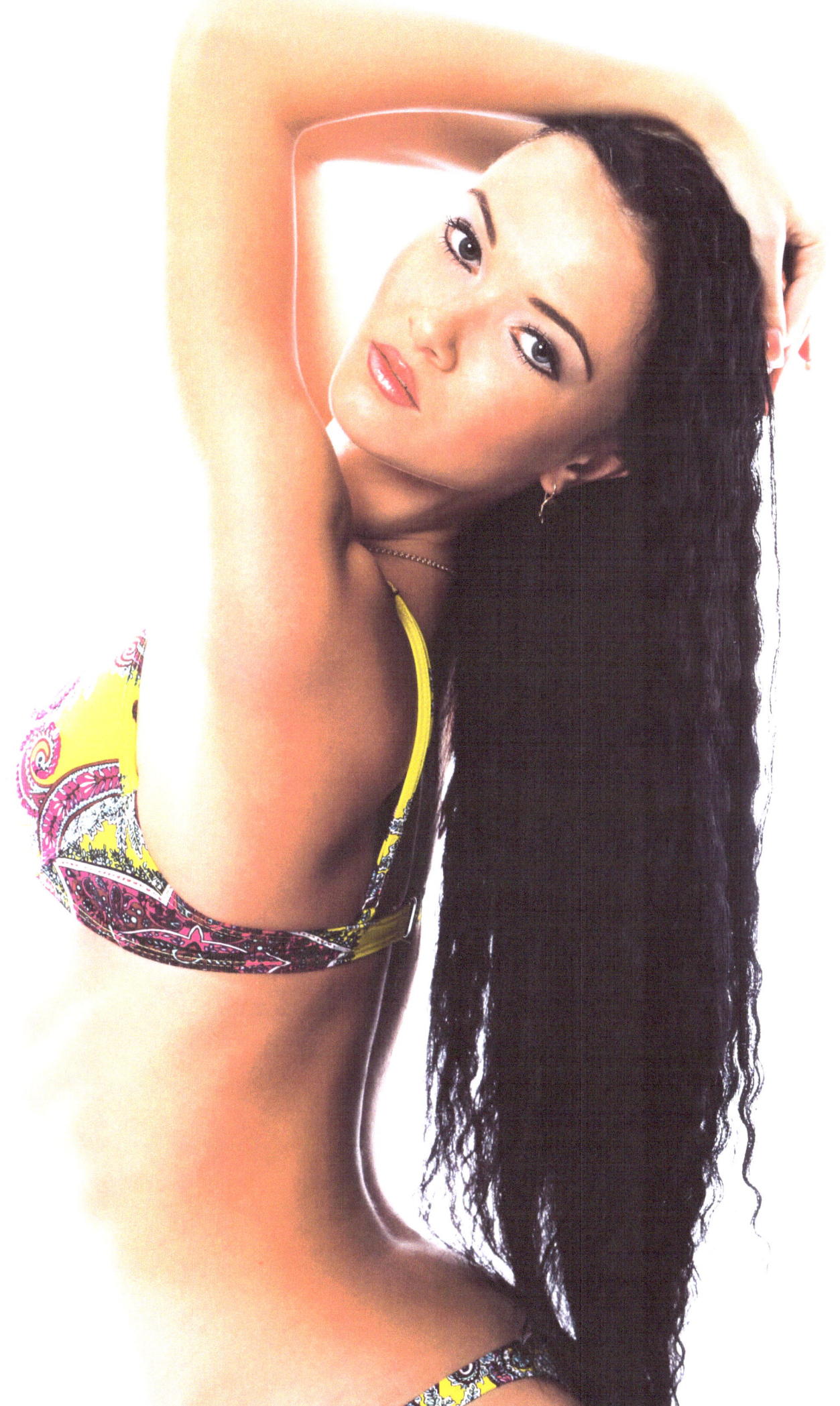

www.ingramcontent.com/pod-product-compliance
Lightning Source LLC
Chambersburg PA
CBHW050418180526
45159CB00005B/2319